WELCOME TO THE WORLD OF
Raccoons

Diane Swanson

Whitecap Books
Vancouver / Toronto

Edited by Elizabeth McLean
Cover design by Steve Penner
Cover photograph by Thomas Kitchin/First Light
Interior design by Margaret Ng
Typeset by Tanya Lloyd
Photo credits: Wayne Lynch iv, 2, 20; Victoria Hurst/First Light 4, 8, 14;
Thomas Kitchin/First Light 6, 12, 22; Jessie Parker/First Light 10; Aubrey
Lang 16; Glen and Rebecca Grambo/First Light 18, 26; Tim Christie 24

Printed and bound in Canada

Canadian Cataloguing in Publication Data

Swanson, Diane, 1944–
    Welcome to the world of raccoons

    Includes index.
    ISBN 1-55110-782-1

    1. Raccoons—Juvenile literature. I. Title.
QL737.C26S92 1998   j599.76'32   C98-910652-7

For more information on
this series and other
Whitecap Books titles,
visit our web site at
www.whitecap.ca

The publisher acknowledges the support of the Canada Council for the Arts
and the Cultural Services Branch of the Government of British Columbia for
our publishing program. We acknowledge the financial support of the
Government of Canada through the Book Industry Development Program
for our publishing activities.

Contents

World of Difference

RACCOONS GROW THEIR OWN FACE MASKS. Dark fur helps hide their bright eyes, making them hard to spot at night. But raccoons can see you well in the dark—if you're not too far away. Their eyes see much better in dim light than yours do.

The first Europeans to spot common raccoons in North America thought they were masked dogs. Most raccoons are about the size and weight of small dogs, but they don't belong to the dog family. They're related to pandas instead.

Raccoons have bushy tails ringed with bands of dark fur. Besides being handsome,

With its thick fur coat and dark mask, the raccoon is a handsome animal.

Well built for running along branches, raccoons live easily in trees.

these tails help the raccoons keep their balance when they walk along tree branches.

Long, sharp claws on their feet make climbing easy. Raccoons can even scamper down a tree headfirst, turning their back feet to the side to grip the trunk. Or they may just decide to jump. They can leap from quite a height without hurting themselves.

On the ground, raccoons are not nearly as nimble as they are in trees. They waddle along on stubby legs, but if they're in danger, they can run short distances. They can also swim well.

Raccoons make great use of their two front paws. They have a keen sense of touch, and their long, slender toes work somewhat like fingers. A raccoon can use these handy paws to snatch clams, pick fruit, flip lids off garbage cans, unlatch picnic baskets—even unscrew jars.

Raccoons that live in big cities often surprise people. Here are some of the reasons why:

- Raccoons go where the food is. One climbed a big construction crane to eat scraps the operator left.
- Raccoons learn to use tools. One broke a window with a rock to get inside a greenhouse.
- Raccoons get caught up in traffic. One was rescued by police from New York City's subway tracks.

Where in the World

WET AND WOODY HOMES ARE BEST—for raccoons. They prefer shady forests and woodlands close to streams, lakes, and seashores. Living near water means living near plenty of food, such as fresh berries and crayfish.

Raccoons feel more at home in the trees than they do on the ground. Thick, high branches make great raccoon rest stops. They're safe places to soak up sunshine or to sleep all through the day. A raccoon might curl up with its legs tucked in. Or it might flop on its back, shading its eyes with its front paws.

From their cozy home, these young raccoons peek out at the world.

5

In cities, raccoons can find homes and rest stops even on buildings.

Most raccoons have several rest stops. Some may be empty woodpecker holes, fox dens, or skunk burrows. The raccoons might have to chew or scrape these hollows to make them bigger. But they usually need a place only big enough for one—except when the mothers are caring for their young, called kits.

Many raccoons live comfortably in towns and cities. They make homes in back yards, parks, empty lots, and cemeteries—almost any place with trees and shrubs. Raccoons get around by slipping through underground tunnels and pipes or traveling along bushy riverbanks.

Different kinds of raccoons live in different parts of the world, but common raccoons live naturally just in North and Central America. They adapt well, so there are still many raccoons around today.

RUNAWAY RACCOONS

During the 1940s, several raccoons were taken from the United States to Germany. There they were raised on a farm for their thick fur, but some escaped.

Today the great-great-great-great-grandkits of those runaways live in Germany, wild and free. A number of them moved into towns, where some people feed them. But gardeners who find raccoons eating their vegetables often wish the animals had been left where they belong.

7

World Full of Food

CORN ON THE COB IS A REAL RACCOON TREAT. And it's easy for raccoons to eat. Using their handy front paws, they can grab a big, juicy cob and strip off its leafy layers. Then they hold the cob—often at both ends—and nibble.

Corn may be a favorite food, but it's not all that raccoons eat. In fact, their menu seems endless. They feed on many kinds of vegetables and fruits. They snack on nuts and gobble up eggs from turtles as well as from birds. They climb trees and steal honey from bees while their thick fur saves them from stings.

For many meals, raccoons head to lakes and streams to fish.

9

Mmm, cereal! Raccoons find plenty of food in cities.

When it comes to meat, raccoons dine on prey as large as snakes and rabbits. But they also pounce on tiny animals, such as grasshoppers, slugs, and worms.

Many raccoons hunt along shores. They might reach out from the edge to grab their dinner, or they might wade or swim in the water. They catch fish, frogs, and crabs, and snatch up shellfish, such as mussels and oysters.

Raccoons are good at hearing and smelling their prey. And they use their paws and nose to feel for food—even in mud or water. Sometimes their rummaging in water makes people think that raccoons always wash their food. But they don't. Raccoons aren't that fussy.

Nighttime is when they usually do most of their eating. If food is easier to find in the daytime, though, the raccoons will be right there.

BACKYARD BUFFETS

Around people's homes, raccoons can sample many different foods. One raccoon sucked syrup out of a hummingbird feeder. Another ate bird seed. It licked its paw, jammed it into the seed, then wiped its paw clean with its tongue.

Three raccoons that spied an apple pie by an open window ate up all the apples, but left the crust. Others have gobbled up ice cream cones, popcorn, even ketchup—straight from the bottle.

World of Words

MANY THINGS CAN MAKE A RACCOON CROON. It talks when it's happy, and it talks when it's mad. Sometimes it talks to meet up with other raccoons.

Kits often cry out with high, trembling voices that can mean all sorts of things. Mostly, they are calling for their mothers, and they're saying, "We're hungry. Come and feed us."

When raccoon kits are well fed and feeling cozy, they lower their voices. They pur-r-r softly. Their mother may purr, too. But if her purring suddenly changes to a short, muffled "Mmm," the kits leap to

Making itself look big and tough, a raccoon barks at an intruder.

13

attention. They know that's a raccoon warning signal. Danger is near.

There's no mistaking the sound of a threatening raccoon. It hisses, snorts, or barks sharply at intruders. Sometimes it does all three. If the raccoon is very angry and ready to fight, it snarls and growls.

**"Mine, all mine,"
this raccoon seems
to say, as it guards
the grapes it found.**

Raccoons often use their furry bodies to help them talk. Their tails whip back and forth when they're annoyed. And when they're making threats, they might drop their heads and lower their ears. They might also raise their backs and tails to make themselves look bigger. By showing their sharp teeth at the same time, they make their threats seem even fiercer.

But if a raccoon senses more trouble than it can handle, it may just lower its body and quietly slip away.

MUSIC THAT SPEAKS

Many animals—including raccoons—respond to the sounds of music. One woman discovered that raccoons often came to her porch or window when she played the piano. Another person claimed raccoons were very attracted to music by a German composer named Johann Sebastian Bach.

Some raccoons like the music on TV. They also peer through windows to watch the shows—especially those with plenty of action.

New World

A KIT DOESN'T ARRIVE IN A THICK RACCOON COAT. At birth, it's just a fuzzy ball, but its mother is ready to keep it warm.

In spring or summer—before her kits arrive—she finds a cozy den. She often picks a tree hole that will shelter her family from bad weather. It must also be a safe place to hide from enemies, such as eagles, owls, coyotes, and bobcats. Inside this tree hole, she might make a soft bed of leaves.

Raccoons that live in the country give birth to up to five kits. City raccoons often have bigger families. Each kit may only be as

Hauling a kit from the water is just part of the job for a mother raccoon.

17

Only four weeks old, this kit is waiting for its mother to return.

long as a chain of two or three paper clips. It weighs no more than a bar of bath soap.

When the kits are born, the mother raccoon licks them clean. Their eyes are shut tight, but the kits cuddle close together. They fill their tiny bellies with warm milk from their mother.

When she goes out to hunt for food,

the mother raccoon stays close enough to hear her kits. That way she can rush home if they need her. If she must move the family to a safer nest, she carries the kits. One by one, she grabs the loose skin on their necks with her teeth.

The kits change quickly. By the time they are about three weeks old, they look more like grown raccoons. Their eyes are open, their face masks are thick and dark, and their tails are ringed. They're almost ready to face their new world.

HOME IS WHERE YOU MAKE IT

City raccoons find strange places to raise a family. They turn up in sewers, attics, and sheds. One family spent winter tucked between the ceiling and roof of a porch. Another climbed the fire escape of a tall building, tore off a roof vent, and settled in. In an empty house, a mother raccoon kept her kits beneath an old bathtub that stood on feet. Raccoons have even lived inside a piano someone tossed out.

19

Small World

PLAYING FOLLOW-THE-LEADER, KITS EXPLORE THEIR WORLD. They start tagging after their mother when they're about two months old. One behind the other, they follow her on short trips.

If the raccoon den is up high, the mother may move her family closer to the ground. Then her lively kits won't get hurt if they happen to fall.

By copying their mother, raccoon kits learn what food to eat and where to find it. They watch her climb trees to nab young birds and slip into fields to snatch corn.

If danger lurks, the kits learn to scoot

Whoops! Even raccoons— especially kits— can slip and fall from trees.

21

A mother raccoon keeps her young kits safely huddled beside her.

up trees. Their mother gets them to safety before she looks after herself. If she can't escape, she fights fiercely.

The kits continue their lessons through the summer. Some spend a few days on their own, feeding by themselves. In many parts of North America, they try to put on plenty of fat. Then they won't have to eat much when the weather turns cold.

Kits often stay with their families during their first winter. Together they curl up and sleep deeply. But on mild nights, they might wake up and head out for a snack, then fall right back asleep.

The family breaks up when spring comes, and the young raccoons strike out on their own. In cities, where there's plenty of food, they grow fast. They often get bigger and live longer than country raccoons. Some might live 10 years; a few have lived to age 16.

PRETEND FRIEND

People at a wildlife shelter were caring for a sick raccoon kit that its mother had left behind. One worker put a toy animal into its cage. The kit pounced on it, pretending to fight. It talked to the toy, making raccoon sounds. It even slept with the toy.

All this playing, talking, and sleeping with a stuffed animal helped the kit practice what it would have done in its own family. It helped the kit grow up as a raccoon.

Fun World

KITS RUN, LEAP, AND POUNCE IN PLAY. That's not only fun, it's the way kits practice skills they use to catch prey. The exercise builds strong back legs, too, and helps keep the kits fit.

When kits—or even grown raccoons—get an animal skin, they grasp it with their teeth and shake it. If they live around people, they might play with a leather glove or shoe the same way.

Raccoons seem to like playing with shiny things, too. They hold metal chains or jar lids in their front paws and turn them over and over.

"Last again," this kit seems to be thinking, after racing its brother up a dead tree.

25

Six weeks old and ready for play, this kit is out to have fun.

Bright colors attract many raccoons. One city kit wandered into a house and climbed inside a playpen. There it rolled and tossed a baby's red and yellow plastic toys.

In zoos where animals can't search streams for prey, raccoons often plunk their food in water. Then they grope around for it, as if they are play hunting.

Raccoons like to slide and splash into water. In a back yard, a pair of kits climbed to the top of a child's slide and coasted down, landing in a wading pool. They must have had fun because they did it over and over again.

One kit was adopted by a pet dog whose puppies had just left her. The kit learned to play with dog toys. Its favorite seemed to be a little rubber football. The kit carried the ball in its mouth as it followed the dog around the yard.

TREEHOUSE SPORT

"Ee-ow-EE! S-s-s-s. Ee-OW!" The noise woke up the neighbors. It was louder than a cat fight—and it was followed by banging and clanging.

As people peeked out their windows, three lively raccoon kits peeked back. They had climbed inside a treehouse where they'd been playing up a storm. First, they'd leaped on each other, pretending to fight. Then they'd rolled a metal pail around and flung toys right out of the house.

27

Index